MOBILE

tunnel

STAPLETON

SPANISH FORT

LOXLEY

DAPHNE

ROBERTSDALE

Fairhope

SUMMERDALE

POINT CLEAR

Mobile Bay

FOLEY

PENSACOLA

WARRINGTON

BON SECOUR

BON
SECOUR
BAY

ORANGE
BEACH

PENSACOLA
BEACH

FORT MORGAN

GULF
SHORES

M E X I C O

Alabama

Florida

JUBILEE!

By Karyn W. Tunks

Illustrated by Julie Dupré Buckner

PELICAN PUBLISHING COMPANY

GRETNA 2012

The word "Pelican" and the depiction of a pelican
are trademarks of Pelican Publishing Company, Inc.,
and are registered in the U.S. Patent and Trademark Office.

ISBN 9781589808805

Printed in Singapore
Published by Pelican Publishing Company, Inc.
1000 Burmaster Street, Gretna, Louisiana 70053

To all the children, past, present, and future, who know the magic of the jubilee.

Caroline inhaled deeply and held her breath as her mother drove through the opening of the narrow tunnel. The two-lane tube that was hollowed out beneath the river provided a passageway across the bay for summer travelers. Halfway through the tunnel, red-faced Caroline sputtered out a forced exhale. Her mother smiled, remembering this impossible childhood game of trying to hold your breath from one end of the tunnel to the other.

Breezing across the causeway, Caroline inhaled the warm, muggy air rolling off the bay. She closed one eye and focused with the other through the viewfinder of her camera as they sped past the people fishing along the bank.

After driving for what seemed like forever, Caroline
spotted familiar landmarks. She read the storefront signs
out loud as if announcing stops on a passenger train.
Another turn and the car followed the winding road that
mimicked the curves of the bay.

Finally, the crunching of oyster shells beneath the tires announced their arrival. Caroline jumped from the car and ran to greet her grandmother. She showed off her camera and asked, wide-eyed, "Grandma! Do you think we will have a jubilee this summer?" Her grandmother hugged her, laughed, and steered them into the house to enjoy the supper waiting on the table.

As the sun began to set over the bay, Caroline's mother said goodbye and headed back home. Caroline and her grandmother walked down to the shoreline. They watched the sun dip down in the sky. Caroline said, "Please, Grandma, tell me again about the jubilee." Caroline's grandmother described the mysterious event.

"Jubilees happen in the early morning hours of the long summer days. The bay shimmers like gold and is as slick as glass." She whispered knowingly, "Sometimes a few anxious crabs will give away the secret by coming to the shore early, even before sunset." Caroline listened intently as her grandmother continued, "The flounder, crabs, and shrimp wash up to shore, as thick as thieves, and they lie there for the taking. But you must watch your step because slippery eels and stingrays come right along with the good stuff."

The next morning Caroline woke up early. She was disappointed that there had not been a jubilee the night before but was excited about her plans for the day. After breakfast, she jumped on the rusty bicycle kept in the garage and headed out to visit old friends. The camera hung from the handlebars, bumping Caroline's knee with each turn of the pedals.

First, she visited Newt and Thelma, who owned the local service station. Thelma pried the cap off a cold RC Cola and scooped full a bag of freshly boiled peanuts for Caroline. Out front, Newt filled the bike tires with air. After catching up on the gossip, Caroline asked, "Have you ever seen a jubilee?" Newt and Thelma looked at one another and smiled. "A jubilee is a wingding of a good time!" Thelma exclaimed. Folks watch for signs of the jubilee and then clang backyard dinner bells to alert their neighbors. Friends enjoy each other's company and share what they catch.

Newt joined in, "The party goes on until the sun comes up . . . kind of like Mardi Gras!" Together Newt and Thelma let out a burst of laughter, and Caroline snapped a picture of them with their mouths wide open.

Next, Caroline rode over to a small, whitewashed church. She parked her bike at the door, stepped inside, and listened as Brother Nathan rehearsed his Sunday sermon. After catching up on the praises and prayers from his congregation, Caroline asked, "Have you ever seen a jubilee?"

415
914
608
617
210

Using the same rhythmic tone usually reserved for his sermons, the preacher began, "Why, yes, I have! Jubilees are a gift from God. When his divine creatures are too fruitful, God stirs up the bay and pushes them ashore, creating a bounty for the brethren. And some mighty fine eatin' it is too, praise God. Why, even the word *jubilee* comes from the Holy Bible!" Caroline snapped a picture of Brother Nathan as he wiped the sweat from his brow.

Finally, Caroline pedaled her bike to Miss Mettie's house. The beloved schoolteacher was reading to the neighborhood children. The story ended and the children meandered home. After catching up on the school year, Caroline asked, "Have you ever seen a jubilee?" The teacher took a deep breath and spoke as if she were standing in front of a classroom of students, "I have experienced many jubilees. Most occur late in summer during the month of August. The eastern breeze pushes in the rising tide, and the sea life swims to shore seeking more oxygen in the water.

However, instead of finding the oxygen they need to survive, the creatures are greeted by jubilee hunters, who happily take them home and eat them for dinner." Caroline snapped a picture of Miss Mettie as she smiled smugly at her own joke.

That night, Caroline fell into a deep, sweet sleep. The faint sound
of a dinner bell found its way into her dream. The ringing seemed
to travel closer and closer and Caroline struggled to wake up.

Suddenly, her grandmother rushed in shouting, "Jubilee! Jubilee! Caroline, wake up. We are having a jubilee!" Caroline jumped out of bed, grabbed her camera, and ran toward the bay, stopping only to ring the dinner bell to alert more neighbors.

Looking toward the water, Caroline could see glowing dots of light from kerosene lamps breaking through the dark sky. Squeals from children and excited voices of grown-ups grew louder as she reached the bay.

At the water's edge, Caroline marveled at the sight before her. A mishmash of creatures lethargically swayed in rhythm with the slow laps of the tide. The shallow waters of the shoreline were overflowing with fish, crabs, shrimp, and stingrays. Caroline tiptoed over the eels that had wriggled ashore, but there were too many to miss. She shuddered as one squirmed out from under her shoe.

Up and down the shoreline, jubilee hunters gigged fat flounders two at a time. The flat fish slapped their tails frantically as onlookers marveled at their size. Along the pier, women leaned over and under railings, reaching with dip nets to gather the sluggish shrimp. The dazed shellfish were an easy catch as they bumped clumsily against the pylons.

Even the children skillfully picked up crabs with their bare hands, carefully avoiding any snapping blue claws. The crustaceans appeared calm, but no one wanted to risk the painful pinch of a crabby crab.

The delicacies were collected in any available container. Washtubs, ice chests, and bushel baskets were filled to the brim. Wet cloths and burlap sacks were draped on top to prevent a get away, but still the flounders flopped noisily and the crabs scritch-scratched the sides as they tried to make an escape.

In the dark, Caroline made out the familiar images of her old friends and snapped pictures as they reveled in the jubilee. For each one, the jubilee was just as they had described it.

Newt and Thelma laughed noisily with neighbors and gave away their supply of shrimp, as if they were the hosts of a party.

Brother Nathan's pant legs were rolled up, and knee-deep in the bay, he shouted, "Praise God," with each wiggling flounder pierced by his gig.

Grasping a blue crab, Miss Mettie gave a science lesson to the children who had gravitated to her side.

As daylight broke, a light rain fell over the bay. The drops hit the surface, gently stirring fresh oxygen into the water. By then, the once-abundant shoreline was picked over like a cotton field full of boll weevils. The remaining sea life was revived and quickly swam to safety in the sandy depths of the bay. One by one, tired jubilee hunters trudged home to ice down their catch.

Caroline, elated and exhausted, walked to the house and crawled into bed. Her grandmother pulled a quilt over her and asked, "Caroline, was the jubilee everything you'd hoped for?" but the answer had to wait. Caroline was already asleep dreaming of her next jubilee.

Glossary

Bankhead Tunnel: The 3,389-foot, double-steel-shell tunnel built in the early 1940s is named for Alabama politician William Brockman Bankhead. The tradition of holding your breath from one end of the tunnel to the other began when drivers became unnecessarily concerned over health hazards from car fumes collecting in the tunnel. This is a game that children still practice today.

Boiled peanuts: This popular Southern snack is made by boiling green (freshly harvested) nuts in salty water for four to seven hours over an outdoor fire. The shells turn soggy and are removed with fingers or teeth, and the nut inside is eaten (usually outdoors, because of the mess). Boiled peanuts are most popular and available from May to November. The tradition of boiling peanuts has been traced back to the Civil War.

Boll weevils: This agricultural pest, no more than one-quarter-inch long, infested cotton crops in Alabama beginning in 1910. The insect destroyed the cotton boll, the seed pod that contains the cotton. The infestation forced farmers to diversify (rotate) their crops, resulting in successful cash crops such as peanuts. As a result, vital nutrients were returned to the soil that had been depleted by growing only cotton. On December 11, 1919, the town of Enterprise, Alabama, erected a large statue in honor of the boll weevil.

Causeway: Mobile Causeway, completed in 1929, connects Mobile to Baldwin County. It is a nine-mile stretch of highway, beginning at the Bankhead Tunnel in Mobile and ending at Spanish Fort. Fishing from the bank is a popular pastime.

Fairhope Avenue: Fairhope Pharmacy, Walkers 5 & 10, and Vicks Barber Shop are the names of actual stores on Fairhope Avenue in 1963. The avenue still offers quaint shops for locals and tourists, and Fairhope Pharmacy is owned by the same family today.

Gig: This is a type of fishing spear that can be purchased or homemade. The end has one or more sharp points, approximately twelve to fourteen inches long, that may or may not be barbed. The gig is plunged down into the flounder, and then the flounder is picked up by holding the gig in place and sliding a hand under the fish.

Holy Bible: The word *jubilee* is referenced in the Bible, and the "Year of Jubilee" is described in Leviticus. "For it is a jubilee and is to be holy for you; eat only what is taken directly from the fields" (Lev. 25:12, NIV).

Kodak Instamatic camera: The Kodak Instamatic 100 was released in 1963. It introduced the easy-loading 126 film cartridge, making photography easier and more accessible. The pop-up flashholder required single-use flashbulbs. In 1963, it sold for $15.95 (more than $100 in today's currency).

Mardi Gras: This celebration has a long, rich history in different parts of the world. The date of Mardi Gras is determined by the Christian calendar. Mardi Gras (French for "Fat Tuesday") began in Mobile in 1830 and continued until the Civil War. The practice of dressing in costumes and parading through the city was resurrected in 1866 by Joe Cain. Today, a number of societies hold parties (Mardi Gras balls) and parade on floats, throwing trinkets such as beads and doubloons to onlookers.

Miss Mettie: This character was created in tribute to Marietta Johnson (1864-1938), progressive educator and founder of the Organic School, which is still in operation in Fairhope today. It is said that the children of Fairhope gravitated to this esteemed teacher and affectionately called her "Aunt Mettie."

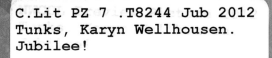

N

W E

S

N

S

BILOXI
OCEAN
SPRINGS

Mississippi
Alabam

TH

PASCAGOULA

ALABAM
POIN

M I S S I S S I P P I   S O U N D

AT
LAND

SHIP
ISLAND

HORN
ISLAND

PETIS BOIS
ISLAND

DAUPHIN
ISLAND

G U L F

O F